Moving Forward

Details of an Autism Journey

Sonya A. Bell

Moving Forward: Details of an Autism Journey

Printed in the United States of America.

First printing: October 2023

ISBN: 9798864358016

Edited By: Tamira K. Butler-Likely, Founder of LikelyWrite

Email:likelywriteediting@gmail.com

Published by: Toccara Nicole, Founder of VOS Consulting and Publishing International

Website: yourauthorsauthority.com

Email: hello@yourauthorsauthority.com

How to contact the author:

Website: beyondradianthc.com

Email: sonyabelltheauthor@gmail.com

Please Note: The author is not a doctor. Please consult your doctor to gain directives on how to address all health issues and concerns.

DEDICATION

This book is dedicated to all the individuals who are parenting a child or children who have been diagnosed with any form of autism. Autism, or autism spectrum disorder (ASD), is a neurodevelopmental condition with a broad range of conditions ranging from challenges with social skills, repetitive behaviors, speech, and nonverbal communication.

As an autism mom, I see you. It is my hope and desire for you to be inspired to move forward with faith; to know that you are not alone.

FOREWORD

"A Journey of Faith and Divine Intervention!"

Within these pages, you'll find a remarkable story of Sonya A. Bell that speaks to the depths of faith and the undeniable presence of divine intervention in her life. It's a story of faith, hope, and the profound impact that faith can have on our lives. It reminds us that even in our most challenging moments, when we turn to God for guidance, we may discover that He is indeed in the details, orchestrating events that lead us toward answers, solutions, and, ultimately, a deeper understanding of His plan. The journey we embark upon in this narrative is one of profound significance.

As you delve deeper into this narrative, it's a tale of a mother's unwavering love, the challenges of raising a child with unique needs, and the extraordinary moments of clarity and guidance that can emerge from the most unexpected places.

In the opening pages, you'll read about a heartfelt conversation with God, a conversation that flowed from a heart filled with gratitude for the gift of motherhood and a plea for guidance in caring for a beloved child. It's a conversation that resonates with anyone who has faced adversity, sought answers, and clung to faith in times of uncertainty.

It's a journey that begins with a pivotal moment, a women's health meeting at church, on a day when the challenges of parenting were particularly heavy. What transpires during that gathering is nothing short of extraordinary, a twist of fate that reveals God's presence in the most unexpected ways. It's a world where hope is tested, and the need for answers is paramount.

This foreword merely scratches the surface of the incredible journey you're about to embark upon. You'll be drawn into a mother's world, a world filled with the complexities of raising a child with unique needs, navigating therapies, and searching for solutions.

- Williamson Sintyl

Global Humanitarian, Author, and Certified Professional Coach at Peakcorp.co_

Table of Contents

Acknowledgments

I appreciate everyone who has been on this autism journey with us. I would like to express special gratitude to the following people:

First and foremost, I would like to thank my sweet husband, Keith, who has been by my side every step of the way. You are the best life partner I could have ever asked for! You are so patient with me and have always been my biggest fan! Thanks, babe, for your love and support.

Secondly, I am forever grateful for our four children, Maya, Keenan, Isaiah, and Elijah (our fourth child who wasn't born yet during the timing of these events). Thank you guys for being part of my purpose in life. I love being your mom. Each of you are truly a gift from God and I'm forever grateful for your presence in my life.

There are three special ladies in my life who I will forever be grateful for: my mother, Valencia Cummings; my mother-in-law, Annie Minor; and my auntie, Willie Randolph. I am grateful for the unconditional love that radiates from each of you.

Lastly, I can't forget my cousin April Vincent Watson. She has always encouraged me to write a book and share my story. Well, I finally did it! Thanks for encouraging me.

I truly am surrounded by loving and supportive people.

I hold deep gratitude to my writing coach, Toccara Nicole. I can't thank you enough for encouraging me to step outside of my comfort zone and share my story.

I am also grateful to my editor, Tamira K. Butler-Likely, for your patience and guidance.

Introduction

We are all impacted by some form of disability. We have a family member, neighbor, friend, coworker, etc., someone we know, who has been diagnosed with a form of disability.

For our family, our second son was diagnosed with autism. Autism, or autism spectrum disorder (ASD), is a neurodevelopmental condition with a broad range of conditions ranging from challenges with social skills, repetitive behaviors, speech, and nonverbal communication.

Our only daughter was diagnosed with attention deficit hyperactivity disorder (ADHD) and a learning disability in math.

Even though I had retired from nursing, in my professional career, my experience had been with adults, not children. I had limited knowledge regarding autism, ADHD, or learning disabilities. That was all about to change!

As a mom living with this, I wanted to do more than just drive my kids to speech and occupational therapy appointments. That was not enough! I needed to do more! I was not seeing progress and that was unacceptable!

Our entire lives changed when I said a little prayer.

CHAPTER 1

Boy, You Hear Me!

"Ike, Ike, Ike!" Now I know that by now that boy heard me calling his name. I'm in the kitchen and he's less than six feet away from me. I asked my husband, Kenneth, "When was the last time you called Ike's name, and he answered you?" He honestly couldn't remember.

An hour later, we were all sitting at the kitchen table—Kenneth, myself, and our three kids—when the doorbell rang. Ike leaps up from the table and runs to the door. Clearly, this boy is not deaf! Although, lately whenever I call his name, he has stopped answering me. This is becoming a habit and I am starting to get concerned.

A few months earlier, after returning home from the doctor's visit where he received the 18-month vaccine (which he received at 20 months of age due to our family moving), we noticed that he stopped responding to his name being called.

Ike is the youngest of three. He's by now two years old and his older sister Michelle is six, and his brother Zac is four. Ike is a calm-natured child, and Lord knows I needed that! His older siblings are extremely active. I actually prayed and asked God for this baby to be calm, and HE answered my prayer.

As a matter of fact, before we knew the sex of the baby, we thought he was a GIRL! Ike was actually my second pregnancy, but our third child. That's because we adopted our first child, our daughter. She was a blessing after three years of trying to conceive.

MORE Babies!

With so many unsuccessful attempts, we decided to adopt. She came into our home at the age of thirteen months old. She was our foster daughter prior to us adopting her. It took one year for the adoption to become final. It was a joyous occasion in our home once she was officially ours!

Funny thing is, a few months after she came into our home as our foster daughter, we found out I was two months pregnant!
(Has this ever happened to you??)

I honestly had no idea that I was pregnant. I had polycystic ovarian syndrome (PCOS), and my OBGYN told me that because I had so many cysts on my ovaries, it would be difficult for me to get pregnant. We were informed about fertility drugs and we tried one round. It was unsuccessful, and I did not want to try it again, it made me nervous. So we were content on adoption.

Digestion Section

Do you have an adoption story or infertility story? If not, perhaps you know someone who has experienced something similar.

CHAPTER 2

Emergency Room Visit

So, I have to share this story of how we found out I was pregnant. Kenneth and I were at my brother and sister-in-law's house with Michelle for the weekend. My brother-in-law grilled chicken and we ate side dishes. After eating, I became nauseous and started vomiting. As if that wasn't enough, I also had diarrhea! I felt awful and thought I had food poisoning! I told my brother-in-law that he probably didn't grill the chicken all the way.

He just gave me that side-eye look like, "yeah right, sis." We were an hour and a half from home, but I insisted that my husband drive all the way to our hometown to drop Michelle off with her baby-sitter and then take me to the hospital. Her baby-sitter was actually her first foster parents (who brought her home from the hospital), so they knew her very well and she was familiar and comfortable with them.

Upon arriving at the Emergency Room, the nurse asked all of the health history questions. I answered them all and then she asked me if I was pregnant. I remember telling her that I was not. I had taken a pregnancy test a few weeks ago and it was negative (like all of the tests I had taken). Honestly, I was so over taking pregnancy tests! They would just get my hopes up, only to be disappointed.

I told her about my PCOS condition. She was very attentive and listened closely to me. They drew bloodwork as well as took a urine specimen. Some time went by, and the ER doctor came into the room followed by my sweet little nurse who had been so attentive to me earlier. Now mind you, my husband is sitting in the room with me. The doctor, with a smile on his face, says to me, "Mrs. Bell, your pregnancy test came back positive... Congratulations!" The nurse had the biggest smile on her face. She also said congratulations and they both exited the room. Now, I am laying there in shock, trying to process what just happened. My husband leans over to me and says, "So what does that mean?"

I looked at him and said, "You're sitting right here, you didn't just hear them say that we're pregnant!" I don't know if he was taking a nap or just in la la land. LOL!

I requested an ultrasound because I couldn't stop thinking about the doctor who told me that I would have difficulty getting pregnant, and we had been trying for three years so ....

So, the ultrasound confirmed the pregnancy and there was no evidence of any cysts. It was a miracle in my eyes. God had removed those cysts and we were about to have two babies in our home...just like that.

Digestion Section

What miracles have you seen in your life?

Ask the Expert

Note: Use this space to write down any questions you may have for your healthcare professional.

Ask the Expert

Note: Use this space to write down any questions you may have for your healthcare professional.

CHAPTER 3

Mama Knows

So, we had a healthy pregnancy with our first baby. We wanted to be surprised and opted to not find out the sex of the baby. I do remember thinking it was a boy, because he was a strong kicker. That baby was active and he wanted me to know it too.

I was correct. We delivered a healthy baby boy. Within a year, we went from no kids to two!

We had always talked about having four kids, so we started on baby number three. We weren't sure how long it would take to get pregnant, since it took three years the first time. Surprisingly, it did not take too long, and I was pregnant again. This time we did not want to be surprised by the sex of the baby. I suspected it was a girl because this baby was very mild mannered and not as active as pregnancy number one. This one had light movements. My other two kids were so busy and all over the place, I prayed and asked God to please let baby number three be a calm, peaceful child.

Tummy Roll

We found out from the ultrasound that it was another boy...so I was wrong. That was fine with me. I just wanted another healthy baby. Although, I did pray and ask God if the baby boy could be calm and peaceful, because his older sister and brother were busy and all over the place. They woke up running and didn't seem to get tired. One thing that they loved to do was to slide down the stairs head-first on their tummy. They would get a kick out of this. They would land at the bottom of the stairs giggling in laughter. Only to bounce up and run up the stairs to do it again. Sometimes, this would continue for hours. You would think it would hurt them, but they loved every minute of it.

So God granted my prayer request and baby number three, who we named Ike, was another healthy delivery. Ike was indeed a calm-natured baby. He was not very fussy and was just a delight. Ike was developing normally, just like his siblings, meeting every milestone appropriately.

By the time Ike was old enough to walk, his older sister and brother had taught him how to slide down the stairs head-first on his tummy as well. Now I had three kids sliding down the stairs. Clearly, they entertained themselves.

Say What?

We moved to a new city when Ike was fifteen months old. After a few months in the new house, we started noticing that Ike didn't seem to hear us calling his name. We also noticed he was playing differently. I would find him lining his hot wheel cars up in a straight row. Not only that, but I would find him in the pantry, lining my canned goods up in a row.

We started noticing that Ike was playing alone instead of with his older siblings. He was getting upset easily. If his brother or sister would attempt to play with him or remove a toy that he was playing with, he got upset and started a tantrum.

So, after a few weeks of this behavior and me calling his name and him not responding, I began to worry. My fear was that he had developed an ear infection and it went unnoticed. I was thinking maybe he ruptured an eardrum or something. I didn't know. Clearly, I was reaching...trying to understand what was going on with my baby. I was definitely reaching for answers because I did not understand why my beautiful little toddler, who at one time would answer me and run into my arms when I called his name, was now silent.

Sidebar: Now I know several moms who can relate to this. Please pay attention to the signs. I recommend praying for guidance.

Digestion Section

What details stood out to you after reading this chapter?

CHAPTER 4

What's up Doc

We took Ike to his pediatrician for a well-child visit. The doctor examined both ears and did not notice anything out of the ordinary. She said everything looked healthy and normal, no infection, no inflammation. Hmmm...this made me even more curious as to what was going on.

I had been told that the Atlanta Area School for the Deaf would do an exam for free. I was still searching for answers, so I scheduled an appointment. I took Ike in for his exam and he passed that test with flying colors! She reported, "no abnormalities noted." Ike could hear better than I could! LOL

Needless to say, my husband and I were puzzled. The next idea was to have him evaluated by a speech therapist. We were curious as to what stage of development he was actually in because at this point, he WAS NOT TALKING anymore. There were no audible words coming from his mouth. He was just babbling.

Interestingly enough, my husband's job was in early childhood intervention. He worked closely with several pediatric therapists. So, he called and asked a colleague if she would evaluate Ike's language skills. After her evaluation, we finally received valid data that indicated we had a problem. This would officially be the start of our journey with autism.

To Rule Out...

Sheila, the speech therapist, called my husband in tears. I mean, literally, she was crying on the phone. She said, "I don't know how to tell you this but, I think you need to take him to be further tested to rule out autism." She was crying so hard and felt so bad, that I felt sad for her. She went on to say that according to the test results she received, his language was on a 13-month-old level. He was two years old at the time of her testing him, so he had regressed severely.

We were curious and wanted a second opinion. We wanted to see if the results would be different, so my husband asked another speech therapist to evaluate Ike. The results were the same, "Take him to be evaluated to rule out autism."

"Autism," this word did not scare me. I just wanted to know what was happening with our son. Give me something!! Our next step was to have him evaluated by a pediatric neurodevelopmental specialist. We obtained the referral from our pediatrician, scheduled the appointment, and drove an hour to Augusta, GA, for this appointment.

Digestion Section

What details stood out to you after reading this chapter?

CHAPTER 5

It's Official Now

Ike and I arrived at the office a little early. We sat in the waiting room, he sat on my lap, and I observed the other moms sitting there ...waiting. I wondered if they were like me, there because they were told to "have him further evaluated to rule out autism." Or perhaps, they had already received their diagnosis, and this was not their first appointment.

After a series of questions from the doctor and her evaluating my son, she invited me back into her office, closed the door, and proceeded to tell me, "Your son does have an autism spectrum disorder."

I remember sitting there in her office, not quite knowing what to think or feel. In a way, glad to finally have a name for what was going on with him, but at the same time, kind of at a loss for words. By this time, he's on the floor mumbling and playing with some toys that she had in her office. At this stage in his development, he had stopped speaking with words and he mumbled. I looked at him, then I looked at her and I asked, "What can I expect from him by the time he's an adult?" I don't think she expected me to ask that question, because she was silent for a few minutes. Then she said, "You can expect some symptoms or no symptoms." *What kind of answer is that?* was my thought. I was at least grateful to finally know what we were dealing with. I thanked her, picked up my handsome little guy, and walked out of her office, passing by the other parents. Wondering how they would take the news, if they were there for the first time.

It's not in my character to accept this type of news without taking further action. That's just not who I AM. I had to continue the process. Indeed, this was not the end, but the beginning.

I asked our pediatrician for another referral. This time it was for the Marcus Institute in Atlanta, GA. The Marcus Institute, now known as the Marcus Autism Center, is one of the largest autism centers in the US.

I scheduled an appointment for a diagnostic evaluation. I was pleased with the office visit, because they spent more time doing the evaluation. They were more thorough in their exam, but it did not change the outcome. They concurred that Ike had a diagnosis of autism. Although, she did say that on the autism spectrum, he was mild-moderate, not severe. By now, we had two speech therapists evaluate him and two doctors who specialized in autism do an evaluation. We were very clear on the diagnosis...autism.

What I wasn't clear on was the next step. I'm grateful for the sense of peace that enveloped me, there was no anger or sense of overwhelm. I never once said, "God, why me?" On the contrary, I kneeled by my bed and said a little prayer.

Digestion Section

Parents, please know that it is OKAY to ask your healthcare practitioner questions. It is also OKAY to ask for a referral for a second opinion.

Your healthcare practitioner is partnering with you on your behalf and/or your child's behalf.

CHAPTER 6

God Stepped In

I had a conversation with God and thanked HIM for blessing me to be a mother. After all, it had taken me three years to get pregnant. I was extremely grateful for my children and then I asked HIM to help me with Ike. I remember saying, "You have blessed me with this child, now I need help."

I have strong faith in the power of prayer. I really felt that God heard my prayer and would guide me. God has been in so many of the details of our journey.

The first detail occurred when I attended a women's meeting at our church that was for women's health. There was a holistic doctor who was invited to speak to the women on women's health issues. To be honest, I wasn't going to attend. It had been an extremely exhausting day.

Ike had several tantrums that day. He was so frustrated and upset at the dinner table that he slapped me! It caught all of us off guard! My son, Zac, immediately came to me and gave me a hug. He gently touched my face, as to comfort me. My husband, Kenneth, picked up Ike to try to calm him, because by this time, he was crying and everything was chaotic! To keep from crying in front of the kids, I went upstairs to my bedroom. My husband got Ike calmed down and then came upstairs to check on me. He insisted that I get out of the house. He was right. I pulled myself together and drove to church to attend this women's health meeting. I had NO IDEA what I was about to walk into!

The room was full of women with familiar faces. The doctor was standing in the front of the room about to start as I walked in. I quietly sat toward the middle of the room. He spoke on several health issues related to women. I just sat there trying to absorb what he was saying, but quietly wondering how I was going to help Ike. Physically I was there, but mentally I was far away. My thoughts were on all of his speech and occupational therapist appointments. Honestly, not feeling as though they were helping him.

By this point he was three years old and the tantrums were increasing not decreasing. He was still nonverbal and not grasping the sign language the therapist was teaching him. Not to mention, we had purchased a sign language DVD that we were all learning so as to communicate with him. The few signs that he got and used were “more” and “please.”

So, during the doctor’s presentation, my thoughts were all over the place. I surely wasn’t mentally present. The hour went by rather quickly, and now we were at the end and it was Q&A time.

Since my thoughts had been on my son this entire time, I raised my hand to ask a question about autism. I asked if he had experience in working with children and autism. Now remember when I said this was the first detail of “God being in the details.”

I wish you could have seen my face when Dr. Rogers told me that he was a DAN doctor. DAN stands for Defeat Autism Now. WOW! Really God, so this is how we are doing this!! I was in shock, my face said it all. I could have flipped all across the room! I was so happy and surprised quite honestly when he said that.

Who’s DAN

The DAN protocol was initiated in 1995 by Dr. Bernard Rimland. It’s an approach to autism treatment that stems from the idea that autism is a biomedical disorder. The protocol focused on addressing autism through biomedical interventions such as nutritional therapies, chelation therapy (removing heavy metals from the body), and hyperbaric oxygen treatments, to name a few. The DAN protocol was discontinued in 2011 by the Autism Research Institute. The reason for discontinuing DAN protocol was partly because the name "defeat autism now" was offensive to some people.

Who would have imagined my day would have ended on such a positive note. After the turmoil of tantrums, I never would have imagined such a peaceful and hopeful end to a stressful day. This was, in my opinion, a "Divine appointment," because God is in the details.

Digestion Section

What details stood out to you after reading this chapter?

CHAPTER 7

One Simple Wish

The following morning, I called and scheduled an appointment. We had an appointment that following Thursday. It was at a medical facility that was an hour away. No problem, the distance was not a factor. I had already decided that I would make a sacrifice to get the help Ike needed.

We arrived at the appointment a few minutes early so that I could complete the paperwork. I was so happy that Ike was having a good day. Partly because he had his green sippy cup. He loved this sippy cup. I diluted apple juice with water and that kept him quiet. He cooperated with the nurse and the doctor.

At this point, my wish was simple. I just wanted the tantrums to stop. Dr. Rogers had a whole page of suggestions. For example, people had suggested I try a gluten-free diet for Ike, but I had not started yet. I didn't know where to begin, until now.

Answered Prayer

I asked and I had received. I had prayed to God to help me find additional ways to support our son, other than speech and occupational therapy. This was an answer to a prayer. Dr. Rogers handed me a sheet of yellow paper from the legal pad that he had made notes on. It was a list of suggestions including nutritional resources from gluten-free and casein-free diets to vitamin supplementation. I was so excited to get started!

During the first visit, bloodwork was ordered. We had to make a separate visit to our local hospital for the bloodwork and they gave me the specimen cup to collect the stool specimen at home. On the second visit, he would discuss the results of the lab work.

Feingold

One of the resources Dr. Rogers shared with me was the Feingold program. I had not heard of this before but I was intrigued. Dr. Ben Feingold was a pediatrician and allergist in California who observed the link between certain foods and additives and behavior. Dr. Feingold developed a nutritional technique that is basically an elimination diet. This elimination diet was a two-phase process. It consisted of removing certain additives, which are: artificial food colors, artificial flavors or Vanillin, and artificial sweeteners (Aspartame, AminoSweet, NutraSweet, Equal, Acesulfame-K, Advantame, Cyclamates, Saccharin, Sweet N' Low, Sucralose, Splenda), BHA, BHT, and TBHQ. We also eliminated sodium nitrite and sodium nitrate from our diet. Also, if you had any non-food item with any of those chemicals, they were to be avoided as well. This was because any artificial coloring, flavoring, or petrochemical preservative that goes in your mouth or on your skin would cause a problem. This meant I was now reading labels on our personal care products as well as our cleaning and laundry products. As a result, we changed our toothpaste to make sure it didn't contain any of those chemicals as well as our body wash, hand soap, dental floss, shampoo, conditioner, etc. I started using laundry detergents that were "free and clear." Those were acceptable to use. This may seem like a lot of work and seem tedious, and it was! But, I would do it all over again, because it was worth it! These habits became a part of our "family culture." It did not matter if we were on vacation or at home, I continued to avoid food and products that contain those above-mentioned chemicals.

Digestion Section

What details stood out to you after reading this chapter?

CHAPTER 8

Food Additives

Since you may not be familiar with some of the additives mentioned above, let me explain a little more. Starting with **BHA**:

BHA (butylated hydroxyanisole) is a petroleum-based food additive. **BHA** was first introduced as a food additive in 1947. It's considered to be a synthetic antioxidant used to prevent fats in foods from going rancid and as a defoaming agent for yeast. It's listed as a possible carcinogen, and it causes hormone disruption as well as harms the reproductive system. **BHA** is commonly found in cereals, gum, processed potatoes, drink mixes, shortening, snack foods, frozen pizza, fast food, and cured meats such as pepperoni and sausage.

BHT (butylated hydroxytoluene) is another petroleum-based food additive. **BHT** was patented in 1947, approved as a food additive by the FDA in 1954, and since 1959 has been on

the Generally Recognized as Safe (GRAS) list. The GRAS list is maintained by the FDA.
BHT is used as an antioxidant in foods, animal feed, petroleum products, synthetic rubbers, plastics, animal and vegetable oils, and soaps. The concerns are based on research with laboratory animals that were given **BHT**, and it caused lung and liver tumors, lung inflammation, bleeding, and liver enlargement.

It's common to find this preservative in dry breakfast cereals, potato flakes, enriched rice, margarine, and food packaging labels.

TBHQ (tert-butylhydroquinone) is another food additive that is on the GRAS list. It's used as a preservative to prolong the shelf life of foods. It's commonly found in Pop-Tarts, Rice Krispies Treats, and Cheez-Its, to name a few. **TBHQ** is known to harm the immune system and it weakens the effectiveness of vaccines.

Artificial Food Colors also known as synthetic colors, synthetic dyes, food coloring, food dyes, color added, and the popular FD&C colors. Food dyes are also made from petroleum. There are nine food dyes that are approved by the FDA; Blue 1, Blue 2, Citrus Red 2, Green 3, Orange B, Red 3, Red 40, Yellow 5, and Yellow 6.

Research shows that artificial colors are associated with inattentiveness, hyperactivity, and restlessness in children.

Artificial colors are found in numerous items such as processed foods, candy, beverages, colored icing, toothpaste, medications, and vitamins to name a few.

Now that we have discussed artificial colors, let's turn our attention to Artificial flavorings. Artificial flavorings also known as synthetic flavoring or artificial flavors, is any non-natural substance that is used to create flavors in foods, beverages, or medications. Manufacturers prefer artificial flavors because it's less expensive to produce. Vanillin is the only artificial flavor that is clearly labeled by it's name.

Petrochemicals

Dr. Feingold specifically mentioned these food additives because they are made from petroleum. Petroleum is a type of petrochemical. Petrochemicals refer to all those compounds that can be derived from petroleum refinery products.

Our community and environment are hugely impacted by the petrochemical industry. The petrochemical industry is responsible for manufacturing many of our everyday consumables such as cosmetics, detergents, fertilizers, food packaging, pharmaceuticals, garbage bags, and as previously mentioned food additives.

We are exposed to these chemicals in different ways, such as being absorbed through our skin, inhaled, or ingested. Petrochemicals affect humans by accumulating in tissues and organs thus causing acute or chronic health problems.

Health hazards associated with petrochemical exposure include but are not limited to; birth defects, skin irritation, brain and nerve damage, liver damage, asthma, cancer, ulcers, allergic dermatitis, and hormonal disorders.

We don't live in a "perfect world", we are exposed to toxins daily. However, we can make the choice to reduce our exposure to toxins. I'm grateful that I was introduced to the Feingold program, it has changed our lives.

Write It Down

With the introduction to this type of elimination diet, it became apparent to me that keeping a food journal would prove to be extremely helpful. As a busy mom of three, it was easier to change my entire family's diet. I did not want to single out Ike and prepare him separate food. This was a family venture. As I started preparing foods according to the Feingold program, I wrote down everything Ike ate as well as all beverages, along with his total intake and output (because I also documented how many times he pooped AND a detailed description of what it looked like). Remember, my background is in nursing, so this did not bother me.

Honestly, the more information the better. This helped me to see which foods were triggering his tantrums and possibly which foods were affecting his digestion. Not to mention, I recorded his sleep and behavior patterns also.

I was open and willing to make the changes to our family's diet because I believed this would help Ike. It's important to be committed to the cause. I AM committed to helping all my children grow and prosper, not just Ike. Sure, it initiated with him, but these nutrition changes ultimately benefited all of us!

Digestion Section

Have you made any changes to your family's diet? If so, what are the changes?

CHAPTER 9

You Are SPECIAL

At the time, my kids were at the ages 7, 5, and 3. They were young enough to eat what I provided and they didn't complain. This was a blessing to have kids that did not complain and a kind, compassionate husband. To make it feel special and fair to the other two children, I planned special "mommy dates" with them individually.

I wanted to see results in Ike so I changed our entire family's diet! Changing everyone's diet made it easier on me, and it was healthier for all of us. Our diet changes included eliminating artificial colors, sodium nitrates/nitrites, artificial flavors, BHA, BHT, TBHQ, MSG, gluten (protein in wheat), and casein (protein in dairy). As you can tell, it was quite drastic! We did this for at least six months.

I didn't feel as though this was a difficult task. Fortunately for me, I enjoy cooking and baking! Most of our meals were whole food based with limited processed foods. The few processed foods were gluten free, organic, and void of the ingredients that we eliminated from our diet per the Feingold protocol (as mentioned previously).

Regarding my special "mommy dates" with the other two children, I would take each child out for a one-on-one pizza date. It was a great time for bonding and let's be honest...we were missing pizza!! Pizza was one of our favorite meals and I had put that item on hold because of the gluten and dairy. It also gave the older children something to look forward to.

Another fun thing we did was to have impromptu park play time. Some days Kenneth would come home early from work, and I would take Michelle and Zac to the nearby park just for them to run around and play. We also went to their school playground on some weekends, and they played on the playground toys. These impromptu play times were so much fun, primarily because they were not planned! Sometimes the most fun is being spontaneous! These were some of the best decisions I could have made! Relationships are important and deserve effort and attention.

Quality time with our kids helps to create a nurturing and loving relationship. It can become easy to devote more time toward the child with a special need or disability because naturally, he/she will require more attention. When you parent a special needs child, it becomes even more crucial to make the other children feel special as well. Parents, make sure you are intentional about creating and following through on the one-on-one time with the other children.

Digestion Section

What do you think about the suggestion of one-on-one dates with your children?

Do you think it's important to schedule bonding time with your children and/or grandchildren?

CHAPTER 10

Results

As previously mentioned in chapter 9, our diet changes included eliminating artificial colors, sodium nitrates/nitrites, artificial flavors, BHA, BHT, TBHQ, MSG, gluten (protein in wheat), and casein (protein in dairy). As you can tell, it was quite drastic! We did this for at least six months. Dr. Rogers suggested we try the elimination diet for at least three months. Unfortunately, he left the medical office during those three months. I did not have another medical practitioner to help guide me for a few months afterward, so I continued the diet. I could tell by Ike's behavior, sleep, and bowel pattern that it was effective, so why stop!

To be honest, after the first week of the elimination diet, I noticed NO TANTRUMS! I wasn't expecting results so soon, and every child will respond differently. Not only had Ike's tantrums stopped, but he was falling asleep easier and staying asleep.

We also noticed our daughter, who had been diagnosed with ADHD, had calmed down. Michelle, our daughter, would literally wake up on SPEED! She was so talkative and always had to be moving and busy doing something. Seldom did she just sit quietly, without talking. After the nutrition changes, she was much calmer. Still talkative, but not like she was before, and she was able to sit quietly and watch a movie without the desire to bounce or crawl on the sofa.

What I also noticed was how the nutrition changes impacted my "neurotypical" kid (Zac). He had no diagnosis and his behavior was better as well. I could tell because my husband had taken Zac to the mall one afternoon for some "bonding time." Well, upon returning home, I noticed how active Zac was. He was jumping around, laughing, and just a little more hyper than I had seen him in a long while. As I got closer to him, I could see that his face was different. He came closer and closer to me, and there it was!! BLUE lips and a BLUE tongue! Obviously, my husband had given Zac money for the candy machine at the mall! I was so mad at Kenneth! So, there was my proof that not just kids who had received a neurological diagnosis benefited from the elimination of artificial colors; all kids benefited.

I was so relieved by the results and how positive it was for all of the children. Every child is different and will respond differently. This was our personal experience with how our children responded to the nutritional changes.

We had also begun to see progress in Ike's behavior. The tantrums had stopped. He had stopped biting people and he had engaged in more positive play with his siblings.

He still got agitated at times when I didn't understand what he wanted. During those times, instead of biting, screaming, or slapping (the slapping only occurred a couple of times), he would use hand-over-hand communication. For instance, he would open the refrigerator and take my hand and place it on whatever food he wanted to eat.

Digestion Section

What details stood out to you after reading this chapter?

CHAPTER 11

Leaky Gut

Dr. Rogers had also diagnosed Ike with a digestive disorder called "leaky gut." This was my first time hearing that term. From what I have learned, "leaky gut" is where the mucosal lining of the intestinal wall has increased permeability, meaning that the intestinal wall has become very thin and "leaky." The intestinal wall acts as a barrier to protect against toxins. However, when the intestinal wall is more permeable than normal, it allows toxins into the bloodstream. Dr. Rogers said that it is common for kids on the autism spectrum to have gastrointestinal issues.

Ike's blood tests confirmed his leaky gut issue. Dr. Rogers shared that Ike's gut lining was so permeable that everything he ate was being absorbed into his bloodstream. This realization explained why it seemed like Ike had multiple food sensitivities.

The lab work also showed that Ike had high levels of *Candida*. Dr. Rogers went on to explain that the high amounts of *Candida* caused leaky gut. If you're curious, *Candida albicans* is a yeast, a type of fungus that lives naturally in everyone's gastrointestinal tract, on the mucous membranes, and on the skin. In a healthy symbiotic balance, there is not a problem with the presence of yeast. (I will refer to the term *Candida* and yeast interchangeably during this chapter.) The problem begins when the yeast overgrows. When the yeast overgrows, it attaches its roots into the intestinal lining. This is how leaky gut is created. This causes the porous openings in the gut lining. By so doing, this allows for the yeast and it's byproducts to escape into the bloodstream. Where it can attack any organ or system in the body.

The overgrowth of yeast thrives in the presence of diets high in refined sugars and carbohydrates, dairy, processed foods, alcohol, and hormones, such as cortisol, that are released when there is a high amount of stress. As a result, excessive cortisol raises blood sugar levels. The yeast doesn't care where the source of sugar comes from, it will utilize the sugar to reproduce itself. And you wonder why sugar has such a bad reputation!

As a result, all of the above contributing factors either directly or indirectly destroy the good microorganisms in our gut, thus allowing yeast to take over.

In Ike's situation, before we made the dietary changes, he ate the typical standard American diet. He loved cheese, ice cream, and French fries, like most kids. He also ate a lot of bananas, which are a high-sugar fruit. This way of eating was part of why the yeast got out of control. As well as the stress from not being able to communicate. Before meeting Dr. Rogers, I didn't realize Ike had a digestive issue. Meeting Dr. Rogers changed our lives!

After doing more research, I discovered that candida overgrowth is associated with countless other health conditions such as ear and sinus problems, upper respiratory problems, fibroids, thyroid conditions, fibromyalgia, lupus, multiple sclerosis, anxiety, depression, autism, and cancer to name a few.

It makes sense how many of the common health symptoms such as fatigue, bloating, brain fog, weight gain, and allergies can be traced back to *Candida*. *Who knew!!*

I hope you're now starting to get a clear picture of how an overgrowth of *Candida* can become such a health burden and is a serious problem in our community! If you have any unexplained health conditions, consider that yeast overgrowth could be the culprit.

Digestion Section

What are your thoughts after learning all of this?

What, if any, changes will you make in your diet and your family's diet?

CHAPTER 12

Let the Healing Begin

The healing started with the foods. We eliminated all gluten, dairy in all forms, along with certain fruits such as apples, pineapples, strawberries, oranges, and bananas. I kept a food journal, so I noticed how his behavior changed after he ate those fruits. He was more active and he giggled a lot when he ate bananas. Other fruits such as pineapples and apples also affected him. It was explained to me that his body lacked an enzyme that was needed to metabolize the fruits. To be honest, it was difficult for me to withhold these fruits from him initially. I could only see the benefits from eating fruits, such as vitamins, minerals, fiber, antioxidants, etc. It was a real struggle for me but I eventually gave in because I wanted him to have the full experience. I focused more on the foods that he could have, such as pears and melons. He didn't seem to mind. Remember, his tantrums had stopped so he was more agreeable.

It's important to keep in mind, that everybody is different, and everybody will respond differently. This was how Ike responded to the nutrition changes. Let's take a look at a typical day of what he ate...

-<u>Breakfast</u>
grits with butter and salt
eggs, scrambled
sausage, no MSG or sodium nitrates/nitrites
water

-<u>Lunch</u>
turkey sandwich on gluten-free bread, NO CHEESE
baby carrots
potato chips, plain
water

-<u>Dinner</u>
baked chicken
white rice
green beans
juice diluted with water

-<u>Snacks</u>
Gluten-free crackers
cup of pears, no sugar added

You would have thought that the dietary changes would have been difficult, but on the contrary, it was more manageable because we all ate the same foods. I did not prepare separate meals. Once I learned which ingredients to avoid, reading labels became easy. Initially, I spent more time in the grocery store because some of that time was spent on the phone. Yes, I called the manufacturers to find out what "natural flavoring" meant. I needed to know because certain food additives triggered my son to be hyperactive. Some "natural flavorings" such as vanilla or natural extracts from a spice, herb, fruit, or vegetables are okay. However, this labeling process also hides additives that are not natural. That's where the discrepancy lies. We discovered that for him, his triggers were also with BHA, BHT, TBHQ, sodium nitrates/nitrites, MSG, and any type of artificial colors.

Hidden Blessing

I was blessed to be able to retire early from nursing to stay at home with my children. My children needed my attention more. Being a parent is already challenging, with special needs children it's more work. There were the usual activities of cooking and preparing meals, driving my kids to school, cleaning the house, doing the laundry, etc. There were extra tasks such as driving the kids to their therapy appointments and special doctor appointments. We had fun times too, such as play dates, zoo trips, park days, and other fun stuff.

Changing our diet was a game changer for our family in a good way. It impacted the kids' behavior for the positive.

Sodium nitrates and sodium nitrites were also food additives that we eliminated. These two chemicals are used as preservatives to prolong the shelf life of food and to preserve freshness. They are commonly found in processed meats such as ham, bacon, jerky, and pepperoni.

Another additive that we eliminated was monosodium glutamate (MSG). MSG has many names and it can be very confusing. Some of those other names are autolyzed yeast extract, yeast extract, and maltodextrin to name a few. MSG is widely used as a flavor enhancer. It's used in meats, gravies, soups, sauces, and so much more! It's a type of excitotoxin and overstimulates the brain. That is one of the reasons it triggers hyperactivity.

We should have a proactive mindset and eat foods to support and strengthen our mind and body. Food can be our medicine and our poison. We get to choose.

Digestion Section

What details stood out to you after reading this chapter?

CHAPTER 13

ROAD TRIP!!!

After months of dietary changes and witnessing the positive behavior changes in our children, we took a family trip to visit my in-laws. They were so excited to see their grandkids and to witness for themselves their transformation! It was a two-hour road trip. The kids were super excited to see their grandma Ann and their granddaddy Jim! To be honest, I was too! I couldn't wait for them to observe the difference in the behavior.

It was extra special because their cousins were also visiting! We all arrived on a Friday evening. Grandma Ann had cooked dinner for everyone. It was a light meal that consisted of hot dogs and fries. They all ate, and their behavior was fine. No changes noted. Saturday's breakfast consisted of grits, scrambled cheese eggs, bacon, and sausage. Everyone ate and there was no change in behavior. However, we didn't make it to lunch without noticing the obvious change! Oh, my goodness!! By noon, Ike was running in circles in the house, literally! My mother-in-law didn't know what to think. She was trying to get him to calm down, but he was in rare form. He was all over the house. I was puzzled at first. I immediately put on my detective hat, so to speak, and started analyzing what he had eaten. Usually, when his behavior changed, I would take a deep dive into his food. Most times, there would lie my answer. This is why keeping a food journal is so important.

Pay Attention

Okay, so I read the labels on the hot dogs, frozen french fries, and ketchup (from Friday's dinner). I found sodium nitrate in the hot dogs. I read the ingredients on the breakfast foods from Saturday morning, and there again I found sodium nitrates in the sausage. My mother-in-law felt really bad, because she thought she had purchased foods that had the correct ingredients. She remembered to buy foods without MSG, but she forgot to also avoid sodium nitrate/nitrite. I reassured her that it was no problem. He calmed down eventually. Usually it takes about 48–72 hours for it to wear off and the behavior to return to normal. It was a learning experience for all of us. We just dealt with Ike's hyperness. It was a reminder that even though his behavior was calm, he's still sensitive to food additives and when consumed, they will trigger unwanted hyperactive behavior. The food additives were removed for several months and reintroduced (unknowingly), and we all witnessed the behavior change within a matter of hours. It was interesting to note that it took less than twenty-four hours for the hyperactive behavior to manifest but takes 48–72 hours for it to disappear.

Your Tribe

If anything, I was extremely grateful that my mother-in-law tried to accommodate us. She has always been extremely supportive! She knew the work I put into making sure healthy, nonthreatening meals were prepared, and she wanted me to rest that weekend and not have to cook. We had a few phone conversations prior to our visit regarding foods and ingredients. It was an honest mistake. I feel so blessed to have such a supportive family. Having a good support system is essential when dealing with health issues of any kind. We need community. We need understanding, patience, and love. We are surrounded by loving and supportive people.

Being enveloped with love and support is comforting. It's especially needed when dealing with kids on the autism spectrum. Sometimes kids on the spectrum get overstimulated in some situations and want to "run." Therefore, they get labeled as "runners." Our son was one of these "runners."

Digestion Section

Identify the supportive members of your "tribe." Make sure they know how much you appreciate their love and support.

CHAPTER 14

Speedy

The first time he ran was when he was three years old in Pre-K. It was during recess, and he was outside with his teachers and other students. It was a special needs Pre-K class; therefore, it was several students and two to three teachers. This class usually went outside first, before any of the other grades would go out. So, they were the only class at recess. On this day, the spring weather was just right for little Ike to want to take off running in the spring air. He started running toward a busy highway. One of his teachers noticed him and kicked off her shoes and started toward him. Thankfully, she caught him before anything happened! He was giggling when she caught up with him. But, it was no laughing matter. He was running straight toward the highway!

The second incident of running occurred at his grandma Ann's house again. It was on a weekend trip to visit their grandparents. It was another trip that included the cousins, and their auntie and uncle were there as well. There were about a dozen people in the house. It was late on a Saturday afternoon. The weather was nice. The weather was always nice when he ran. The kid was smart, he never took off running on a rainy day.

He knew how to unlock his grandparents' door, and off he went! We didn't realize that he wasn't playing with the other children until we heard a knock at the door. A tall, thin, elderly gentleman asked my mother-in-law, "Does he belong to y'all?" He was referring to Ike. There stands Ike holding onto the gentleman's hand, looking so tenderly up at his grandmother. We were completely shocked! All of us thought, how in the world did this child escape the house and none of us knew!

During this time, he was four years old and nonverbal. He let go of the gentleman's hand, smiled, and walked back into the house. Needless to say, that was the last time that happened...at her house. After that incident, she changed the locks to be childproof.

So, I wish I could say that he didn't run anymore. The third time this occurred was at our home. I wasn't home on this particular evening. I was at a church committee meeting. I was only twenty minutes away. Kenneth was home with the three kids.

I received a phone call from my husband saying to me, “Don’t panic, but I can’t find Ike.”

I said, “What do you mean, you can’t find Ike! Have you called 911?”

He said, “Not yet, I’m going to look for him some more, before I do that.”

I panicked! I abruptly left my meeting and drove toward my house as fast as I could! The entire time I was driving, I was praying. Praying that Ike was safe. All I could think about was the fact that my baby couldn’t talk. He couldn’t communicate to tell someone where he lives. What if he reaches the main highway, which is a very busy street? What if someone picked him up and kidnapped him? All of the “what ifs” played through my mind. I was about five minutes from home when my husband calls me to say, “I found him!”
Wheww!! “Thank God!” is all I could say. My husband proceeded to tell me where he found him. Ike was five houses down, playing in our neighbor’s vans. Notice that I said, VANS. She had two vans in her driveway, and he had opened all of the doors in both vehicles and was running in and out, in and out, giggling to his little heart’s content. Meanwhile, his parents are FREAKING OUT!!

My neighbor was clueless. She didn't have any idea that he was helping himself to her vehicles as a self-made playdate. She was really sweet about the entire ordeal. She was just happy that we found him...safe. So were we.

Kenneth explained that he was upstairs running water for Michelle to take her bath. Ike and Zac were playing downstairs...or so he thought. When he returned downstairs, he noticed he didn't see Ike. He asked Zac, "Where's your brother?" He shrugged his shoulders and said, "I don't know. I thought he was playing." Kenneth realized that the back door leading to our deck was unlocked. He told the other two kids to stay inside while he went outside to look for Ike.

The first place he looked was in the woods behind our house (poor thing, he got into some poison ivy!). When he didn't see any sign of him, he walked toward the front of the house. His white truck was parked with locked doors and no sign of him there either. He thought that would have been where Ike was playing because he was fascinated with cars and trucks.

Kenneth then walked to the end of our driveway and said a silent prayer. He prayed for direction. He wasn't sure if he should go left or go right. Our neighborhood was large, and he didn't want to waste time searching in the wrong direction, so he said a little prayer. He felt inspired to go left, so off he went. His first stop was at a new home under construction, where he asked the workers if they had seen a little boy walking alone? Unfortunately, there was a communication barrier, and they did not understand what he was asking. In fear of wasting any more time, he continued on his way. He was walking in the direction he felt led toward, cell phone in hand, just about to dial 911, when he spotted Ike! His heart was so happy! He ran toward him, heart pounding from so many emotions. By this time, the neighbor had come out of her house. Kenneth explained to her what happened, and she was so kind and grateful that he was safe and that nothing happened to him. So were we!

Digestion Section

What would you have done differently in those situations?

Are you the type of person to remain calm or do you tend to panic in stressful situations?

CHAPTER 15

Too Much!!!

Ike had sensory overload. He could not tolerate loud noises. They overwhelmed him and he would start screaming and place his hands over his ears. So, getting a haircut was a major ordeal. The buzzing noise and the vibration of the clippers sent him into a screaming fit! My husband tried to cut his hair and that was a disaster. He cried and would not sit still long enough for it.

Another incident of him exhibiting signs of sensory overload was on the Fourth of July. We took the kids to watch the fireworks. Well, as you can imagine, that did not go over so well. It was a complete failure on our part. During this time, both Ike and Michelle covered their ears and started screaming. Kids on the autism spectrum typically have sensory issues. They can't tune out certain sounds. It's like they have little antennae and pick up every sound and vibration. Whereas someone without autism would probably not notice certain sounds and it is not a bother. A person on the autism spectrum tunes into every little detail and this can be overwhelming. They tend to get overstimulated rather quickly. Our son could not tolerate fireworks, haircuts, or movies. We decided that I would stay home with Ike and Michelle, and Kenneth took Zac to certain events such as Fourth of July fireworks. It made for a great father-son outing for those two.

Another observation with Ike related to sensory issues was that he couldn't walk down a hill. Instead, he would get down on his knees and crawl. Then he would stand up and begin to play. There was a playground we visited that had a slight incline. He did not walk down the incline like the other children. He crawled downhill. Also, the swings were off limits for him. Trying to put him on a swing triggered an emotional meltdown. He did not like having his feet off the ground.

Don't Bother Me

Socially, at the playground I often had to restrain him either in a stroller or hold him in my arms. This is because sometimes he would hit other children. He wasn't an aggressive child; he was just frustrated that he could not communicate with his peers. He saw his brother and sister playing and having fun. He would often do fine when it was just the three of them. If another kid came along, I had to restrain him because he would not want anyone else playing with his siblings. He wanted his brother and sister all to himself.

This wasn't just at the playground; he was like this at home with other kids. There was an incident with him and my friend's daughter. The little girl was sitting on the couch watching a movie, and he walked up and bit her on the shoulder. She let out a scream and I knew it had something to do with Ike. Unfortunately, he didn't have many playdates.

His older siblings had playdates that were scheduled outside of our house. Thankfully, this all changed as we changed our nutrition habits.

Digestion Section

Have you ever noticed your child becoming frustrated in certain situations? If so, what was your experience like?

CHAPTER 16

Supplements and Tests

Dr. Rogers got us started with the diet changes along with starting supplements such as probiotics and calcium and magnesium chewables. Prior to the probiotics, Ike's stool pattern was inconsistent. He would go from constipation to loose stools. Dr. Rogers was the first holistic doctor we worked with. He was extremely knowledgeable and got us started in the right direction. Unfortunately, he moved out of state shortly after we started seeing him. We would have followed him if it wasn't so far. We returned to the clinic after Dr. Rogers left to visit with the new doctor. He was a cancer specialist and was not a good fit for us, so we discontinued the clinic's services but continued with the nutrition and supplement recommendations.

He did a lot during the short time he was our doctor. He ordered a blood test to test for MMR (measles, mumps, rubella). It was called an

MMR Titer test. It's a blood test that checks for antibodies to those three diseases (measles, mumps, and rubella). Dr. Rogers also ordered a blood titer test for DPT. It's a blood test that checks to see if an individual has been vaccinated against or previously infected by diphtheria, tetanus, and pertussis. I was happy that Ike didn't fuss much when the nurses drew his blood. I was even more happy when the results showed that he had more than enough antibodies. Dr. Rogers said that it wasn't necessary for him to be vaccinated against those disease.

Touchy Subject

The debate of vaccinations is heavy and complicated. I respect the opinion of others. I believe that everyone has their personal story. This is ours. My husband and I observed that Ike stopped talking after he received the 18-month scheduled vaccination. Although, he didn't receive it until he was about twenty months old, right before he turned two. This was because we had moved from one city to another. Our pediatrician was about thirty miles away and quite frankly, with three kids, I just waited. I delayed the pediatrician's visit due to the stress of moving. Our older two children had received their vaccines without any problems. We didn't anticipate any issues.

Ike had been developing normally up to this point. He had reached every milestone without delay. He had a small vocabulary of words, made great eye contact, and engaged in play with his siblings. Needless to say, after Ike's autism diagnosis my husband and I made the decision NOT to vaccinate him anymore. Like I said, this is a sensitive topic, and we were firm in our decision. We were blessed with an understanding pediatrician who did not try to pressure us regarding the vaccine issue. She verbally explained the reasons for vaccinations, we listened and respectfully DECLINED. There was a "refusal to vaccinate" form that I signed. The pediatrician also signed it and we had it notarized. This one piece of document was all that was required for his admittance into school. (Check with your state guidelines. Each state is different).

Very Observant

Kenneth and I noticed Ike playing alone, not engaged in play with his siblings. As a matter of fact, if his brother moved one of his Hot Wheel cars, he had a fit.

I noticed him being quieter. When he spoke, it was echolalia (repetitive words or phrases). He would lay quietly on the carpet lining up his Hot Wheel cars in a single-file row. I would walk into the pantry and notice that my canned goods were all in a straight row. He would be standing there arranging them when I walked in.

I don't think that the vaccines caused our son to become autistic, although I believe it was a trigger. I had been in waiting rooms where other moms would speak to this. They talked about how their child changed after receiving vaccinations. That their son or daughter stopped speaking and became nonverbal.

Maternal Heartache

It was a hard pill to swallow, so to speak. To be honest, it hurt very deeply to think that an action on my part had anything to do with him becoming nonverbal and being diagnosed with autism. Honestly, I know that I did not do anything to cause this, but I still felt responsible...in a weird sort of way. Perhaps, if you are a mom of a child who has been diagnosed with autism, you may understand how I felt.

It was hard mentally and emotionally. I missed the child who would look me in the eyes and kiss me on the lips, the child who would run and wrap his arms around my neck, the child who enjoyed sliding down the stairs head-first on his belly with his siblings laughing all of the way. I missed that child. This was an emotionally difficult time for me, and I didn't let anyone know. I kept those feelings in my heart. I prayed to God because that's how I handled my problems. I turned to HIM and leaned on HIM. I knew that God would provide the peace I needed so badly. I was reminded that "with God all things are possible." I knew that everything would be okay.

Digestion Section

Do you have a similar story of how your child had a vocabulary and then just stopped talking?

CHAPTER 17

Good Things Continue

Our second detail of "God is in the details" occurred one day in the pediatric therapy waiting room. I was waiting for Ike and Michelle to come out of their therapy session. Mandy was another mom sitting in the waiting area for her son to complete his session. We started conversing about how both our sons had been diagnosed with autism. Similarly, they both were also nonverbal. Mandy was very helpful. She had already changed her family's diet. She recommended certain gluten-free foods her kids liked. That was a huge help to me! I was so thankful that she was willing to share those details with me. Even the smallest details, such as her sharing healthy, tasty snacks, made me happy!

The best part was when she shared her story of how a naturopathic doctor in Atlanta had helped her son speak again! Mandy's son was a few years older than Ike, and he had lost his vocabulary just like Ike!

Energetic Experience

She said her name was Dr. Terrie. She was a registered nurse and a certified traditional naturopathic doctor. I got her contact information and called her for an appointment. Within a few weeks we were sitting in Dr. Terrie's office. This truly was a blessing because after Dr. Rogers left, we didn't have a holistic practitioner.

Talk about prayers being answered!! This was how Ike's healing journey continued. I'm extremely grateful for her knowledge, patience, and guidance. Ike was nervous and you could see it in his little eyes. He looked up at me, hesitantly, as he sat in my lap. He was noticeably apprehensive.

Dr. Terrie performed a bioenergetic assessment (BEA) on him. This was my first experience with this type of assessment. She explained that a BEA is a very informative tool that utilizes a computer-based system of testing to measure pathways of energy, which are called meridians.

These meridians flow through the body. I learned that energy readings can indicate if the organs are in an acute inflammatory state or a degenerative state. On a daily basis, we are exposed to toxic influences such as bacteria, viruses, parasites, molds, fungi, pesticides, vaccinations, heavy metals, food additives, and industrial pollution. The wonderful and amazing aspect of the BEA is that it identifies any of the imbalances that may be caused by the above-mentioned toxins. This assessment is very individualized and Dr. Terrie was able to create a care plan that was specific to help our son.

During our first appointment, Dr. Terrie was able to confirm that the leaky gut issue had healed. I was beyond excited to learn such news! All the hard work and dedication of changing our family's diet had paid off!
I had suspected that the gut was healing because his stool pattern had changed. He was having regular bowel movements. There wasn't an inconsistent pattern of constipation and diarrhea.

Dr. Rogers was not able to test Ike's hair because it was too short. Had his hair been long enough, Doc was going to order a hair analysis to be done to check for heavy metal toxicity. Well.... just another reason I was so pleased with Dr. Terrie and the BEA. She was able to check for heavy metal exposure. The results showed that our son had toxic levels of lead and mercury! The results also showed several nutritional imbalances.

Dr. Terrie was amazing! Her patience and concern felt genuine. After a while, Ike was starting to get restless and squirmy in my lap. This was because when administering the BEA, she used a manual instrument to touch acupuncture points on the hands and feet, both right and left side of the body. The manual instrument measured the energetic pathways of each organ and system in the body. This was a necessary part of his exam. It took about an hour and Ike was beginning to get restless. She was prepared because she pulled out an iPad and he watched cartoons until she finished.
God has definitely been in each detail of our journey. Meeting Mandy in the waiting room of the pediatric therapy office and sharing information about Dr. Terrie with me was a GAME CHANGER for our family!! We implemented every aspect of the protocol.

To address Ike's nutritional needs, we adjusted the diet again. The results showed specific foods that were more tolerable for him and which foods he should avoid. That was helpful information. To address the heavy metal toxicity, she recommended homeopathic remedies that were in the form of liquid drops.

Luckily, they tasted good, and he didn't mind taking them. I think he thought they were a treat because he would open his little mouth when he saw me coming with the blue bottle (they were in blue glass bottles). So, I had absolutely NO PROBLEM giving him this supplement.

This protocol went on for three months and then we went back for a reevaluation. We repeated the BEA and Dr. Terrie printed out the report at the end of each visit. We would see her every three months for her to evaluate. At each appointment we saw improvement in the heavy metal numbers decreasing and healing regarding the digestive and neurological systems. It took over a year before the test results showed no indications of lead or mercury toxicity. It was also helpful to have information on which foods he could reintroduce back into his diet. Eventually, after Ike's gut healed, he was able to tolerate gluten and some limited dairy. The gluten had to be organic, but he was able to eat it again. We continued to see Dr. Terrie about once a year. If I had questions in the interim, I would email her. Dr. Terrie was indeed a blessing.

Digestion Section

What details stood out to you after reading this chapter?

CHAPTER 18

Happy Progress

We continued our journey of healing. As a family, we were so happy to see Ike happy and playful again. He was still nonverbal, but he had found a way to communicate with me, even if it was hand-over-hand communication. He was pointing more, which a lot of kids on the spectrum do not do. The tantrums disappeared too, which was my original prayer request. Remember, I prayed and asked God to "please stop the tantrums."

God answered my prayer and He continued to show up in the details.

Playful Pat

The third detail was meeting our wonderful, talented, skilled occupational therapist (OT). Her name was Pat, and my husband introduced me to her. She was a colleague that had impressed him with her talent to help kids speak again. Which you would think would be results that you would see from a speech therapist (ST), although she was not an ST. She was so good that there was a waiting list to see her. We didn't have to wait too long before the initial evaluation. Ike was four years old by this time.

Pat had a special way of connecting with kids. He had seen about three speech therapists in the past and was seeing one at the time that we started seeing Pat. Although the other therapists were good at what they did, Pat was different.

During Pat's evaluation, it seemed like they were just playing, when she was actually testing him. She used many different instruments that measured different skills. He still had the blank stares, echolalia, and trouble following directions. His attention span was poor, and she had to call him back to focus numerous times. She challenged him in ways that promoted growth. Some of the reasons she treated him were related to sensory integration issues.

She Knows Her Stuff

Sensory integration disorder is a neurological disorder where the brain is unable to interpret certain information from the body's sensory systems. The body's senses include taste, smell, touch, hearing, and sight. A person can be impacted by one sensory area or all. People that are impacted by this are usually overly sensitive to certain stimuli that wouldn't bother most people. Remember back in chapter 15 I mentioned how Ike could not tolerate loud noises, haircuts, etc.? Well, it's sometimes described as the brain having a traffic jam.

Ike seemed to enjoy his sessions with Pat. It was worth the two-hour commute to her office. We drove one hour there, and it was an hour home, therefore, a two-hour commute. My daughter, who was four years older but had developmental delays, was also her client. So, it was really a good use of my time.

Some of Ike's sensory integration issues were described earlier such as his difficulty with loud noises, like the Fourth of July fireworks, or the laser show at Stone Mountain. Another example is that he didn't like piggyback rides. He couldn't tolerate having his feet off the ground. This was also known as gravitational insecurity. We just got used to him behaving this way. We thought it was part of autism.

Therapy Tools

As his OT sessions continued, we would be introduced to the weighted-blanket concept. The therapeutic use of a weighted blanket helped calm him down when he got overstimulated and became anxious. The deep pressure of the blanket has a calming effect on the nervous system. I witnessed this several times. As soon as Pat placed the blanket on his shoulders or lap, he relaxed and was able to complete the task she initiated for him to do.

Pat had the blanket for use during his therapy sessions. For home, his grandmother sewed together some weighted bean bags. They were helpful at home to place on his lap when he was restless. It was nice to have this tool for home use.

Pat started using a protocol called Therapeutic Listening with Ike. She explained that Therapeutic Listening utilized organized sound patterns, inherent to music, to impact all levels of the nervous system. Such as to increase attention, balance, body awareness and control communication, social engagement, and organization of sensory input.

We were so blessed that Pat had specialized training for this type of program. She started at the center, and we did it at home on the days that Ike did not have therapy. We invested in the at-home program, which included a pair of high-quality HD500A Sennheiser stereo headphones, which were designed specifically for use with the Therapeutic Listening system.

There were also various kids' tune music on CD that he listened to.

I was surprised when he allowed her to place the headphones on his ears. The weighted blanket helped calm him down. After he got used to the headphones, it was not a problem for me to place them on him at home. Typically, he wore them on the ride to his special needs Pre-K school. That was a twenty-minute ride that we only did once a day.

Digestion Section

What are some of your key take-aways from this chapter?

CHAPTER 19

Mama's Experiment

I wanted to see if Ike's teachers would notice any difference in his behavior. I purposely did not tell them that we were trying a new type of treatment. Typically, in the school setting, when he got overstimulated, he would run around the classroom in circles and he would do the same in the cafeteria. As a matter of fact, him running around the cafeteria became a problem. They eventually had to restrain Ike in a Rifton chair, which was a chair with a safety belt restraint. It prevented him from running as a safety measure.

A few months after Ike starting Therapeutic Listening, his teacher told me that he was calmer in the cafeteria. She also noticed him sitting during the entire duration of circle time in the classroom setting. Usually, he would get up and run around the classroom during circle time. After a few months of Therapeutic

Listening, the running around stopped! That was music to my ears. I shared with her what we were doing in therapy and at home and she was pleasantly surprised!

I am grateful for being introduced to this alternative solution. I am open to trying new things, especially when it comes to helping and supporting my children.

What Say Ye of Therapeutic Listening?

It was evident that the Therapeutic Listening was helping Ike with the sensory integration issues, not just at school, but at home as well. He was able to tolerate a haircut without crying and trying to jump out of his dad's arms. He was able to walk down a hill, instead of crawling! It was amazing to see the progress in him.

Pat explained that this program, when used in combination with other sensory techniques, would help improve certain skills such as focus and attention, oral motor skills and articulation, social skills and communication, and many more.

I understood why she was so popular. No other therapist had ever shared this technique with us. It was another GAME CHANGER!

Digestion Section

Are you open to alternative solutions?

CHAPTER 20

Mama Is Working

With Ike in Pre-K and the other two children in elementary school, I decided to take a part-time, work-from-home job. I became a community resource advisor for foster and adoptive families. It helped that Kenneth and I were Michelle's foster parents before we adopted her. Ike was only at school for half a day, so it was great that I was able to get some work done from home while he was at school. It allowed me the mental space to focus on something else. Mamas need to know and understand that it's not selfish to want to work.

This job was primarily done remotely, but it required me to host community workshops once a quarter in the Atlanta region. I was also required to attend monthly in-person staff meetings and trainings.

None of which I objected to. I was in a position where my husband's work schedule was flexible. Therefore, he was able to carpool the kids to and from school when needed.

It allowed me time to interact with other adults. It was a good opportunity for me to utilize my interpersonal skills and to operate in my zone of genius. I enjoyed planning parties, so when I was required to plan the community workshops, it felt like party planning, and I enjoyed that!! They gave me a budget to work with, and it was completely my event. I was allowed the freedom to be creative. My colleagues and I attended trainings once a quarter, usually out of town and requiring one overnight hotel stay. After being at home with the kids for several years, it was nice to get outside of the house every few months or so. It gave me a mental break and the kids an opportunity to bond with their dad.

By this time, Ike was almost five years old. His behavior was so much better, communicating primarily with hand over hand and pointing. He had also started saying a few words, such as "cookie," "hot dog," and "nuther car" (he was trying to say "another car"). I think it's funny how most of his words were related to food.

My Faith Is Strong

"Faith can move mountains" is one of my favorite sayings. I remember one day my sweet mother-in-law asked me, "How do you know this diet is going to work?" My response to her was, "It has to." My faith is strong. I pray hard and mighty. I believe that God hears and answers prayers. I don't know when and in what way He will answer, but I believe that He always responds. God never ignores prayers. He has infinite goodness and mercy, and He is always with us. Typically, it's us, humans, who turn away from Him. I'm so grateful that I had enough faith to say a little prayer when we got the official diagnosis of autism. I simply said, "Lord, you have blessed me with this child, now I need help."

God heard and answered my prayer. One day I was in Atlanta for a staff meeting when I received a voice message from my husband to "call home." That's never a good message. So on my first break, I stepped outside the building and called home.

He was so eager with excitement, and said, "Guess what?" Ike looked at him and said clearly, "I want sausage." I was so thrilled! I started crying with happy tears, because my baby said a complete sentence and he made eye contact while saying it. I was on cloud nine when I walked back into the building. Everyone could see the obvious JOY written all over my face. My supervisor asked what was going on? I shared with her what my husband had just told me. She also started crying! It was indeed a happy, memorable moment. I can't lie....I had a second thought of "I missed it! I missed his first sentence!"

I quickly dismissed that negative thought. I was not going to allow anything to dim the light that was shining down on my family. I can't begin to tell you how happy I was to see him starting to communicate.

I didn't miss the second sentence. He said, "I want toast." We were so happy that he was able to verbally communicate his needs. As a matter of fact, we were so happy that he was finally able to ask for what he wanted, that we gave him almost anything that he asked for. LOL

It was beautiful to see Ike truly begin to explore the world around him. For instance, one day in the car, he wrapped his arm around his brother and said, "My Zac brother." At the same time, he told on his brother. He started saying, "Zac pinch." No longer were his siblings able to get away with misbehaving.

My favorite thing to hear him say was, "I want Mommy." Or the time I walked in the door from work, and he said, "Mommy home!"

Every person that has autism will have a different experience. Not all experiences have a happy outcome. I am aware of that. I am extremely grateful for our autism journey.

Friends

Along Ike's journey with autism friendships were formed. Kids on the autism spectrum typically struggle with social interactions, therefore friendships are often difficult. In the first grade, Ike met DJ. DJ became one of Ike's best friends! DJ did not see a disability. He was patient with Ike and modeled appropriate child play such as sharing and taking turns. Ike and DJ had many play dates together. When Ike was eight years old, he was baptized. It made Ike so happy when DJ and his mom, Rosie attended his baptism!

(Sidenote: as a mom we just want our kids to form healthy friendships. We want them to feel accepted and included.)

Life is about making choices, and we chose to "move forward." We're moving forward in forming connections, learning, growing, and staying encouraged! Moving forward is nonnegotiable for us. We continue to "move forward" in our daily quest to conquer autism.

Digestion Section

How did this chapter impact you?

ABOUT THE AUTHOR

Sonya Bell resides in Georgia with her husband, Keith, and their four children. Sonya graduated from Georgia College in 1995 with a Bachelor of Science degree in nursing. She worked as a home health nurse for a few years before making a career shift. Once starting a family, Sonya knew immediately that she would be needed more in her home. The
couple have two kids diagnosed with special needs. A son diagnosed on the autism spectrum and their daughter diagnosed with ADHD and a learning disorder.

Sonya has become passionate about educating parents about the role nutrition plays with behavior and focusing issues. She decided to return to school after over thirty years to become an Integrative Nutrition Health Coach. She is now the CEO and owner of Beyond Radiant Health Coaching, LLC.

At Beyond Radiant Health Coaching, Sonya teaches parents and educators how to connect the dots between food and behavior. Her goal is to educate and empower her community; so, they are equipped to make better health care decisions. Some of her services include virtual health coaching, virtual and in person workshops, as well as grocery store tours.

For more information visit her website, www.beyondradianthc.com

Made in the USA
Columbia, SC
14 November 2023